# Batik

# Batik

designs

materials

technique

**Sara Néa**

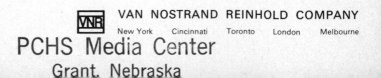

**VAN NOSTRAND REINHOLD COMPANY**

New York    Cincinnati    Toronto    London    Melbourne

This book was originally published
in Swedish under the title
*Vaxbatik* by I. C. A. Förlaget,
Västerås, Sweden

Copyright © Sara Néa and
I. C. A. Förlaget, Västerås, 1970
English translation © Van Nostrand
Reinhold Company Ltd, 1971

Library of Congress Catalog Card
Number 76–156130
ISBN 0 442 05941 8 cl.
ISBN 0 442 05942 6 pb.

Photography—Bo Kågerud,
Göteborg, Berlingske Forlag,
Köpenhamn
Ostra Foto AB, Norrköping

This book is set in Univers and is
printed in Great Britain by
Jolly & Barber Limited, Rugby
and bound by Richard Clay (The
Chaucer Press) Ltd, Bungay,
Suffolk

Published by Van Nostrand
Reinhold Company, Inc.
450 West 33rd St, New York,
N.Y. 10001
and Van Nostrand Reinhold
Company Ltd
Windsor House, 46 Victoria Street,
London S.W.1

Published simultaneously in
Canada by Van Nostrand Reinhold
Company Ltd

16   15   14   13   12   11   10   9   8   7   6   5   4

# Contents

# Introduction

Batik is a resist dyeing process. It consists basically of making designs on textiles by isolating parts of the fabric with melted wax, dyeing the whole fabric and finally removing the wax to reveal the undyed pattern. To make a design using more than one color the process is repeated, waxing different areas. The origins of batik are unknown. Fragments of batik work several thousand years old have been discovered in various parts of the world but it is thought that the craft originated in south-east Asia, probably in Indonesia.

The most famous batik work is Javanese. The ancient crafts of Java all have characteristics in common and their designs reflect their culture and religion. Each district also has individual characteristics of color and design which make it possible to determine exactly where each piece of work comes from. Colors varied originally because the dyes were made from the vegetation to hand and this varied throughout the island. Today although synthetic dyes are used the color traditions have lingered on. Basic designs and shapes evolved separately from region to region and the positioning followed strict rules which the batik artist could only vary in detail. The work was used first and foremost for wearing apparel such as sarongs, shawls, headscarves and kerchiefs of all kinds. A batik sarong takes a considerable time to complete, measuring as it does some 4 to 6 yards long. Even today

Opposite
*The Garuda bird (the wing-span is about 12 inches); late nineteenth-century Javanese batik.*

batik is proudly worn, especially at ceremonies and festivities, and is something of a status symbol. One glance will show the worth, the richness of detail, beauty of color and skilful workmanship, of the garment.

At the end of the nineteenth century printing block batik was started in Java chiefly to bring the price of batik work down. Designs made using this printing technique sought to emulate work executed with the traditional "tjanting" as far as possible. Today machinery mass-produces many of the ancient designs and these mass-produced articles are to be found all over the world. A connoisseur, however, finds little difficulty distinguishing between the mass-produced and the genuine article.

Samples of Eastern batik work were brought to Europe by

*Typical Javanese diagonally striped design from the end of the nineteenth century.*

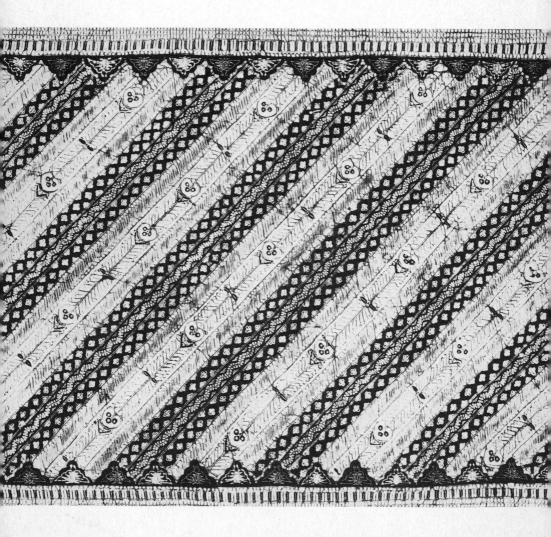

*"Murugan."* A god from southern India who is always depicted riding on a peacock. Here he has his wives Walli and Deivanai with him.

வள்ளி திருமணம் தீபரஸா

*"Family in the garden."*

ஜோஸ்பின்

Dutch colonists in the seventeenth century, but it was not until the nineteenth century that the craft started to win attention in this part of the world. In this century it has grown considerably in popularity, particularly in Scandinavia, and has found a new foothold in India with the establishment in 1965 of a batik industry in Madras. The industry, employing women completely new to the craft, has won wide acclaim for its vigorous, colorful work executed in a bold primitive folk-style far removed from the Javanese traditions.

*Effective batik in cotton.*

*Child's dress in light and dark blue.*

# Ideas for batik work

*Batik is very suitable for party dresses: the short dress is in satin and the long one in linen.*

**Clothes and accessories** Jackets, shirts, skirts, blouses and aprons are all easy to make and allow plenty of scope for the imagination. Outer garments in wax batik may be lined and waterproofed to make them more serviceable. Accessories such as hats, caps, shawls and handbags, collars and cuffs all lend themselves to batik work. Clothes can be brightened up with batik pockets, fichus, scarves and trimmings. Ready-made garments, preferably in some light pastel color (but not non-iron or minimum-iron materials) may also be decorated. For these it is essential to choose very simple designs: collars and pockets, pleats and gathers can interfere with the waxing process. Alternatively, with so many simple patterns readily available in the shops, why not make your own clothes?

*Batik is easiest to execute on a small scale so it is excellent for children's clothes.*

*Decorative cotton pinafore.*

12

A small apron with three kittens.

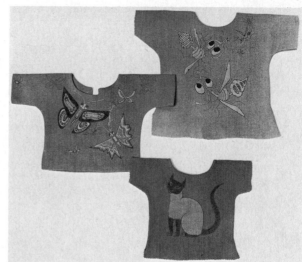

These little children's shirts are in cotton jersey. They were dyed only once. After de-waxing the details in black were hand printed in using a color-fast dye.

Batik silk scarf.

Left top
*Despite the irregular pattern, this tunic in pure silk gives an impression of harmony.*
Left centre
*This is suitable for wearing with trousers but it could also be lengthened into a dress. The matching bag helps to coordinate the design.*
Left bottom
*A comfortable leisure-wear model in denim with an original and simple design.*

Above
*Ideas for designs.*

**Articles for the home** Batik can be a great asset in home decoration (see illustrations on pages 16–19). Table-mats and table-runners, cushions and similar small items are ideal for beginners. Waste-paper baskets, photograph-albums, telephone-directory covers can all help to brighten up the home, or serve as useful presents. Nor, where necessary, is it difficult to mount the material: it can easily be folded over at the edges and gummed down. Book-covers can be much improved by the addition of foam-rubber linings. Small containers can be transformed into decorative jewelry- or glove-boxes. Chair- and stool-covers, blinds, tea-cosies (with foam-rubber lining), mirror-frames (with a cardboard underlay) and lampshades are also good choices for batik work.

Generally speaking all batik work is shown to best advantage if illuminated from behind in some way and the finer the weave the more attractive is the result. For this reason window-panes make effective display-panels for more artistic productions of the genre. In such cases the measurements are reduced and the work is stretched over a square or circular wire frame; the frames may be adorned with glass or wooden beads.

It is best to practise the craft before attempting curtains, table-cloths and similar large projects. Waxing is most easily carried out using the printing block technique (see page 52) and this method is suitable for large projects. Brush batik (see page 44) can be used to good effect if the design is not too fine for a broad brush.

*"Safari." A design to use as a wall-hanging or cushion-cover. Note the symmetry of the figures.*

"Horses." Stylistically executed animals lend themselves admirably to batik.

"Compass rose." The shape of this design could be adapted to larger scale models.

This is an excellent pattern and design for a tea-cosy. The design lends itself to interesting variations.

"Pyramids." This cloth has been given two dyeings. The repeat motif lends itself to reproduction on larger scale models.

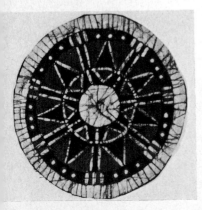

*A batik blind gives individuality to a room.*

*Three table-runners "Snow crystals," "Fighting cocks" and "Sunflowers".*

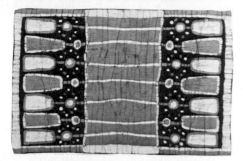

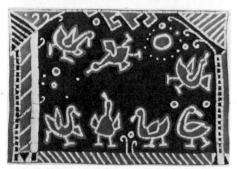

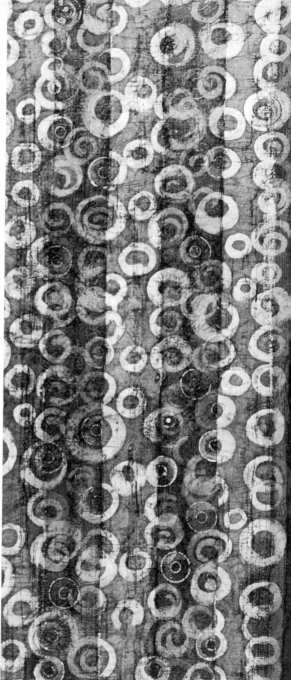

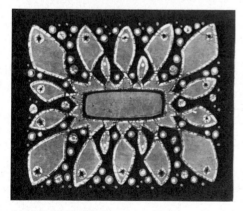

Above *Tray-cloths and table-runners are suitable projects for beginners.*

Right *A pleasing restrained design for curtains.*

# Which materials to use

The choice of material depends on the type of dye used. If a color-fast result is required the choice is limited to natural vegetable-fiber fabrics, for example, cotton, linen, jute and satin because color-fast dyes will not work on anything else. Artificial silk, and synthetic fabrics of the nylon type, are therefore unsuitable, as are natural and synthetic mixtures, also cotton jersey, because the stretching interferes with the wax process. Pure silk, on the other hand, can be used, though with certain provisos (see page 94).

The chemicals used in the processing of certain fabrics (non-iron fabrics, for example) can prevent the dye from penetrating properly and no dyeing can be 100 per cent effective unless the finish has been removed (boiling removes most finishes). If you suspect that a material has been chemically treated it is advisable to test a trial strip first. A strong starch will also interfere with the dyeing process and materials so treated should also be well boiled in a soapflake solution. All materials, with the exception of satin should be boiled before waxing to clean them thoroughly and allow for shrinking. Satin, because it cannot tolerate boiling, should be washed in hot soapy water.

The material used does not have to be white unless you require especially pure colors. A pastel-colored material, say a light gray, will appear as a subdued and soft gray where it would otherwise have been white. Remember that this same gray will also affect, to some degree, all the other colors.

Batik is usually worked on thin cotton material but attractive clothes can be made from poplin, batiste, silk or from fabrics with a raised weave such as piqué. Fabrics with a raised weave are, however, a little more difficult to wax. For winter clothes the lighter materials can be set aside in favor of flannelette, thicker satin, brushed cotton. The material used should preferably be as fine-spun as possible and bleached. The finer the material the more easily the dye can penetrate the fibers. Also, coarser spun fabrics need more dye and more wax and this increases the cost as well as adding to the work of de-waxing. Loose-spun materials with irregular thread thicknesses (cross-stitch canvas, for instance) are only suitable for large patterned work, as in curtains. Linen and unbleached calico are also suitable for curtains. Some materials dye more evenly than others. Linen and silk are better than cotton (poplin excepted) and other mercerized fabrics. Pure satin, with its glossy surface, dyes beautifully.

# Essential equipment

## The following are essential

Batik wax and waxing-pan. Batik dyes. Brushes. "Contact" or "Fablon" for stencils. Frying-pan for printing blocks. Tjanting (dropper). Scissors. Pen and red crayon. Drawing paper for designs. Carbon paper for copying. Thin foam rubber for lining. Tubs (one for dyeing and one for rinsing). Teaspoons; spoons for stirring. Corks. Apron and rubber gloves. Newspapers. Iron. Soapflakes.

## Useful but not essential equipment

Water-colors. Charcoal. Graph paper (for designing). Scotch tape ("Sellotape"). Pipe-cleaners (for block printing). Thimbles (for block printing). Clothespins and twine (see information on wax and tie-dye batik; page 90). Candles (stearine; for drip batik). Waxed shelf paper (for lining). Artists' stretchers. Blunt nail (for pattern-drawing). Detergents. Chemical scale. Fine sieve. Thermometer (up to 170 °C). Clock. Salt. Vinegar.

Note: A centigrade thermometer is preferred for working with wax.

# Work procedure for wax batik using color-fast cold-water dyes

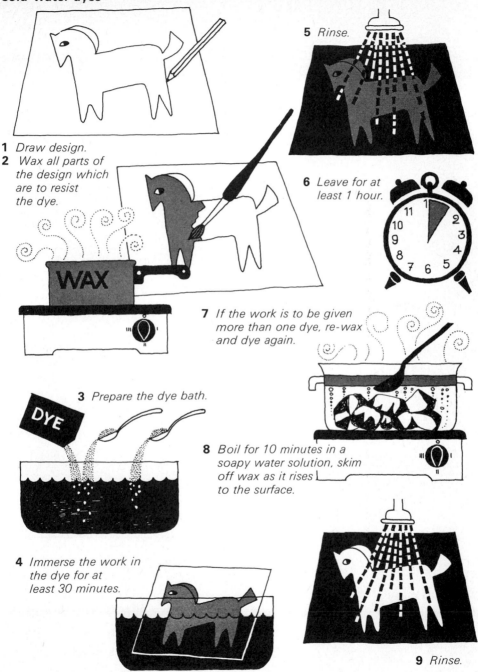

**1** *Draw design.*
**2** *Wax all parts of the design which are to resist the dye.*

**WAX**

**3** *Prepare the dye bath.*

**DYE**

**4** *Immerse the work in the dye for at least 30 minutes.*

**5** *Rinse.*

**6** *Leave for at least 1 hour.*

**7** *If the work is to be given more than one dye, re-wax and dye again.*

**8** *Boil for 10 minutes in a soapy water solution, skim off wax as it rises to the surface.*

**9** *Rinse.*

# Creating designs

The shape of a design in batik is influenced by the particular medium and technique used. The four principal techniques— brush batik, tjanting batik, printing block batik and stencil batik (see illustrations on page 25) are discussed in separate chapters, though in practice designs are almost always executed in a combination of brush batik and one or more of the other techniques.

## Think in batik

You can either follow set rules in working out a design or use your imagination. Figures can be drawn from life, they can be stylized or built up from geometrical figures. To give a pattern coherence and fluidity of line it is best to draw as though using a tjanting or brush, rather than a pencil. In the preliminary sketch use either a soft pencil and red crayon or charcoal and draw on white paper or directly on to the material. By shading the first area to be dyed in red, and the areas to be given the blend color in black, the design stands out more clearly. If you make a mistake, a soft eraser will rub out the pencil marks on the material, and the other pencil marks will disappear in the de-waxing process. Dress designs are often best made direct on to the material and preferably on a living model. In this way it is easier to get some idea of how the dress will look, especially when the wearer is moving about.

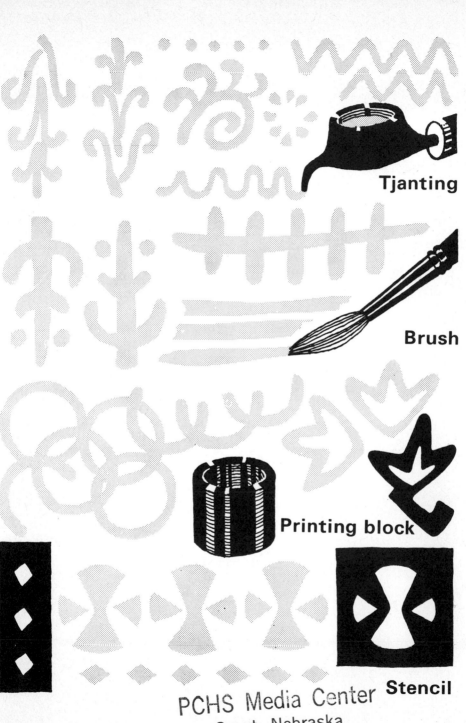

Tjanting

Brush

Printing block

Stencil

PCHS Media Center
Grant, Nebraska

There will be a great difference in the appearance of the design depending on whether use is made of (i) the tjanting only; (ii) the tjanting and the brush; (iii) the brush only. The tjanting produces fine lines which can be made into fish-scale patterns, curlicues, zigzags, spirals, feathery or starry backgrounds, to mention but a few. Tjanting batik has a character all its own, and the "drop" effects so typical of this kind of batik can only be produced with this tool. Brushwork designs are broader and coarser—no lines are much less than $\frac{1}{8}$ inch in width. Whatever the tool, however, broad, straight, even lines are difficult to make and long lines are best broken up with checks, spots, zigzags or similar devices. For the same reason a circle is easiest made by joining two half-moons, and a rectangle is usually more successful if drawn with slightly concave or convex sides. In nature we do not find straight lines so that even if a truly regular design is being followed slight deviations need not constitute a fault. It is in just such irregularities that handmade articles differ from the machine-made perfection of goods off the assembly-line.

If you do not trust the skill of your hands and prefer to use stencil or printing blocks, construct them bearing these considerations in mind.

### Breaking the design into parts

When viewed from a distance a good design must give the over-all effect of a balanced and harmonious distribution of shapes and colors. It may still resolve itself into a pattern largely composed of stripes or spots but there should, nevertheless, be a general impression of balance and unity. Only after the main features of the design have been worked out will it be possible to consider the details. However beautiful these may be individually, without a basic underlying design the essential unity will be destroyed. Oriental mats provide excellent examples of skilful composition in this respect.

Before drawing the design make a small-scale sketch (see diagram on page 27) reducing, say, 50 × 25 inches to 5 × 2$\frac{1}{2}$ or 25 × 12$\frac{1}{2}$ inches. Draw in the details last. For small articles the design in the sketch and the final pattern will follow the same lines but if the original is very much larger than the sketch you will probably have more background to fill in. The choice of color is very important indeed in relation to the design. Try to "think in color" from the very beginning and bear in mind the effect color blends will have on the finished design.

If you are a complete beginner and unused to waxing or handling dyes, choose a large pattern on a small article for your first attempt, for the joy of working can easily be over-clouded by fears that the finished work will be a failure. The harder the task the more important it is to make a full-scale sketch in the actual colors to be used and this is particularly true of any project that is likely to be time-consuming. Such preliminaries will save time in the end *and* give assurance that the final result will be satisfying. If you are undertaking an ambitious piece of work it is wise to get some idea of the final outcome by making a much smaller model using the same dyes and a section of the background detail, and noting the precise details of the dyes and amounts used.

If you are impatient by nature and feel advance planning is tedious and unnecessarily time-wasting, here is a word of advice: execute a few, not too demanding, items; carry out the waxing and dyeing processes without following any predetermined plan. You will find that as your experience increases so too does your interest in advance planning.

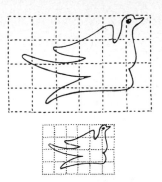

*A small design is easier to enlarge if it is first squared up.*

## Basic designs

Most designs are composed of a regular basic pattern worked out symmetrically over the entire surface of the article. A striped design is made by using horizontal, vertical or diagonal lines. Combined vertical and horizontal lines or diagonals give checked designs. A rayed effect is achieved by working outward from the center to the edges. A circular design is made by taking the center-point and describing various larger circles each with the same center. It is quite possible to combine certain basic designs and elaborate on these using the whole space (see diagrams on page 30). Attractive basic designs can be made by folding paper or material in complicated arrangements and following the creases. Square paper is easiest to work on, particularly if you are planning repeat designs. Even if you are intending to make an irregular design it is still a good idea to plan how the space is to be utilized and the figures positioned. If you do not the composition can easily become chaotic and unbalanced.

Chemicals in the dye may obliterate the pencil-marks, but it is rarely necessary to re-draw entirely if at the planning stage you include small details in white wherever these seem most appropriate in the design and use them as points of reference for selecting the areas to be re-waxed after the first dye.

Remember that the design should tally with the measurements of your material and that the material should thus produce a very different impression from that of a patterned fabric bought by the yard. If it does not, you are losing one of the particular merits of handmade designs.

## Finding ideas for designs

Every modern design is a link in a chain which leads back to the very first patterns of primitive man. Without many sources of inspiration it would be impossible to create satisfying designs and even the most skilful of artists never ceases to study the many designs that he finds in the course of daily life. Be keenly aware, then, of your environment. Draw inspiration from both modern and historical textbooks on, for example, embroidery or tapestry. Cultivate a feeling for form and color

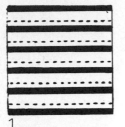
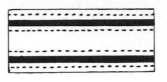

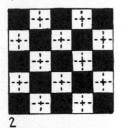

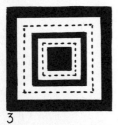

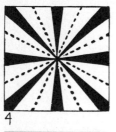

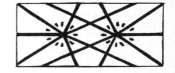

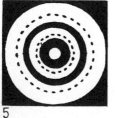

*Examples of basic design shapes:*
*(1) Stripes; (2) Checks; (3) Borders; (4) Rays; (5) Circles.*

and try to adapt designs to your own individual style of work. Most good designs in any medium can be adapted to batik work. The more you study the easier you will find it to make individual adaptations and arrive at a truly personal style— and this will lead to an ever-increasing interest in creative designing.

You do not have to be a skilful artist to create a good design. There are, after all, so many different ways of setting about it. Be wary only of too ambitious projects and of extremely irregular designs. Very often the simpler a thing is the more beautiful it is. It is unwise to begin by composing a small pattern in the center of the material, or high up in one corner— divide the total area into its component parts and proceed on the basis of this in a planned and orderly fashion. Usually a decorative framework is enough to mark out the various sections. Alternatively, the whole area can be used for positioning figures to best advantage, or again the shape of the design may emerge as the various sections are given different colorings. Start by building up your design from the basic shape variations shown in the diagrams on pages 32–33.

## Geometrical figures

Attractive designs can be built up from simple geometrical figures. It is a good idea to use the "variation method" (see page 32). Take, for example, a square—then make a rectangle from this either by dividing it into two or by placing two squares alongside one another; make a triangle by bisecting the square diagonally, and a circle by using one of the sides of the square as the diameter of the circle, and so on. As the figures all possess common features they are easy to combine whether you are composing an entire pattern or just a border.

## Paper patterns

**Cut-outs** Another simple way of making designs is to use a paper cut-out (see diagrams on pages 34 and 36). This is made by folding a piece of paper a couple of times then cutting out various shapes (for best results cut away nearly half the paper). Even if the design created cannot be used in its entirety it can often be adapted.

**Paper shapes** Cut a rectangular piece of paper into different width strips, horizontally, vertically or diagonally. Replace all the pieces and re-form the original figure, then pull it apart again to produce greater and smaller gaps—or try standing the pieces on end or at quite different angles (see diagrams on page 35). This type of design is particularly suited to stencil batik.

Alternatively, using this method, cut, say, a rectangle into a number of wide strips or make a simple paper shape. Cut out a few simple shapes along the edges and open out on an underlay so that the two cut-outs face one another mirror fashion (see diagrams on page 37).

Two batik silk scarves based on geometrical designs.

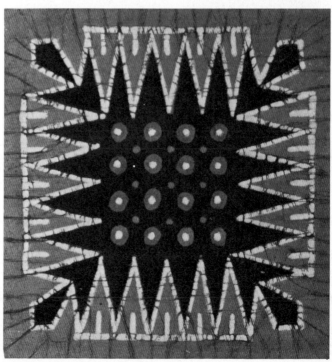

Left *Designs which are simple to enlarge.*

*Variations on basic
shapes lend themselves
to modern designs. These
are all based on triangles.*

**Colored paper shapes** Another source of inspiration is to
use paper designs in various colors (see diagram on page 34).
For instance, fold a piece of white paper over several times and
cut out from it a simple shape that will be easy to wax (this will
give you several pieces). Similarly, fold a colored piece of paper
several times and cut out a rather larger shape from it. Set the
pieces against a dark background so that they form a pattern.
Where the white and the colored papers touch one another the
white paper should always be placed on top (because this will
be the first to be waxed). It may be necessary to alter the cut-
outs a little here and there or add more shapes, but continue
in this fashion until a satisfactory result is obtained. From a
pattern made in this way it is easy to work out how the design
is to be waxed before the first and second dyeings. This method
of designing is also particularly suited to stencil work.

### Repeat, symmetrical, positive and negative designs

Repeat designs are those in which a figure (regular or
irregular) is repeated over and over again to cover a whole
surface (see diagrams on page 38). A symmetrical design is
one which can be divided into a number of similar sections. A
repeat design may be built up by working horizontally, vertically or in both directions simultaneously. If the design is
repeated mirror fashion then a mirror symmetry is obtained.
The repeats may even follow one another in a circular fashion.
If the design is turned through different angles then entirely
new patterns will emerge. Because of the way in which a

symmetrical design is obtained it will always be well balanced but it can easily become monotonous. This monotony can be relieved by, for example, coloring the repeats alternately blue and yellow. Naturally, a symmetrical design will become more interesting if two different repeats are used, especially if one is rather larger than the other.

The spaces between repeat designs frequently make designs themselves. These are called the "negative" figures and the repeats themselves are called the "positive" figures. The closer together the positive figures can be placed the more attractive the result will be. A particular choice of color may even reverse the effect and make the negative figures look positive—if, for instance, the background is stronger in color than the designs superimposed upon it.

*These four squares show how to build up patterns by varying a basic shape.*

*1 Squares and circles.*

*2 Parallelograms.*

*3 Rectangles and ovals.*

*4 Triangles.*

33

### Transferring the design

Very few designers, however skilful they may be, set about creating something in batik without first sketching a few lines on the material to give the general idea of the composition. Even experienced designers normally work from a color sketch. It is best to draw on the material with a piece of soft charcoal as this is easy to remove if you have second thoughts. The batik work itself is not affected by the charcoal which disappears completely during the de-waxing process. For most batik work the waxing is not begun until the complete design has been accurately transferred on to the material (apart from any very simple details which can be waxed free-hand).

The transferring can be executed in various ways. As a rule the design will have been drawn on paper to a fairly small scale and details of color and dyeing time worked out. If the design is simple but has, for example, a more elaborate figure repeated in the border, then copy the elaborate section full size on to paper and use it for each of the repeat figures in turn. If the material is fine enough for the design underneath to show through then use white paper and black pencil. A design which has to be copied can be traced on transparent paper (for instance, greaseproof paper). This makes it easier to ensure that the design has been correctly positioned. For tracing it is best to use dressmakers' carbons, which have a gray-black graphite surface (the marks made by this will disappear after washing). If using other types of carbon paper make sure that they are not indelible.

Always secure the carbon and design firmly to a smooth surface—it slips easily during the copying process. If the design is being transferred on to any especially thick material pin another carbon on the back so that the design is reproduced

*Paper in different colors has been used to produce this batik design. It is easy to see where the first waxing was executed, which areas were left white and which were waxed after the first dyeing.*

For paper shape designs it is unnecessary to make
elaborate shapes as a simple cut-out will produce a
delightful design and a few strips will produce innumerable
patterns. The examples shown here, for instance, have all
been made from a $\frac{1}{2}$ inch wide strip cut out zigzag fashion.

35

These three designs have all been made with the help of paper cut-outs. If such a cut-out is used to build up a repeat pattern many variations are possible depending on how the repeat is executed. Color variations will also ring the changes.

there also as the wax may well not penetrate all the way through in which case it will be necessary to wax the back also.

A good way to copy a repeat design is to cut a stencil from transparent plastic, place it over an underlayer of foam rubber and prick around the outlines of the design with a needle, then place the stencil on the material and rub it with a little bag (made from a square of nylon stocking) containing powdered charcoal (see illustration on page 39). For simple designs a stencil showing only the more important guide-lines in the pattern may be enough. Place the stencil on the material and rub over the holes with a piece of charcoal.

For copying very large designs it is well worth while setting up a viewing-screen. The simplest method is to place a piece of glass horizontally between two tables and set a lamp underneath. The glass must lie quite flat—if necessary books can be placed under the one side to ensure this. The design is set on the glass and the material spread over it. When the lamp is lit, and the rest of the room left in darkness, the design can be seen through the material even if it is quite thick. For smaller designs a window-pane, with the help of daylight, will serve the same purpose. In this case it is important to make sure that the design is very securely fastened on to the material to prevent it slipping out of position while the copying is being carried out.

If a design cannot be copied in this way (if it is taken direct from a plate for instance) use tracing paper or cellophane and a ballpoint-pen instead. If your paper design is going to be used a number of times, protect it by placing transparent paper over the design. The transparent paper can be replaced when it wears out. A fresh sheet placed over the design each time it is copied ensures that nothing has been omitted from the design during the copying.

All sections of the design to be dyed should be shaded in lightly with washable red crayon and the sections to receive a color blend should be shaded in with a soft pencil or charcoal

*The "positive" and "negative" sides of a cut-out can be used to build up a good design. Make a simple symmetrical drawing, cut away half of it and work with both cut-outs.*

37

Variations on a repeat
design. The widely
differing effects which
can be achieved using
the same basic design but
changing its position can
be seen clearly from these
examples.

(see below, right). This systematic preparation of the design has two advantages: firstly, you can check that the design has been thought out to the last detail before embarking on the waxing process (especially if the measurements differ from those of the original design); secondly, a shaded design is much easier to wax.

The material itself can sometimes help with the design. If, for example, your pattern has stripes running with the weave you will not need to copy these because the threads can be used as guide-lines. The distances between the stripes will need to be marked out, however, and "X"-marks along the left-hand side will usually suffice for this. If the material is fine-spun it is simple, and quick, to fold along the line of the stripe. If the stripes can be made to follow the creases made by folding the material in half, and then in half again, and so on until the correct number of stripes has been produced, this too will simplify matters. For checked materials repeat the folding at right angles to the original folds. For square or rectangular designs these crease guide-lines should also suffice.

Finally, however you copy the design, check that the material has not been pulled or stretched out of true—if this *has* happened you will see that the threads are no longer running vertically and horizontally at right angles. The horizontal threads (weft) should be very carefully examined for these are the ones that can very easily lose their correct alignment. Always cut or rip across the material horizontally, even if this appears to make the material look lopsided—pull at it vertically to straighten it.

Left *Stenciling a repeat design. It is often simplest to transfer a design on to the material if the stencil is made of transparent plastic and the outlines are pricked out with a needle, then rubbed over with a cloth bag containing powdered charcoal. The design will emerge as the powder comes through the holes.*

Right *It is easier to visualize the finished batik if whatever is to be dyed first is shaded in red crayon, and the areas to be given the blend color are shaded in pencil or charcoal.*

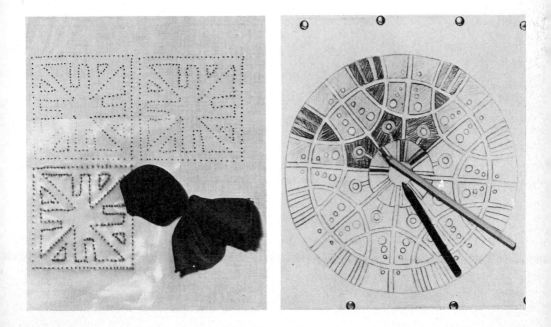

# Waxing

A satisfactory batik wax can be made by melting together one-third beeswax to two-thirds paraffin-wax, or equal quantities of beeswax and paraffin-wax. Paraffin-wax by itself can also be used, but this gives rather too brittle a surface and once heated is so fluid that it is difficult to ensure that the material is covered well enough to resist the dye. The same applies to stearine-wax. Pure beeswax is highly malleable but expensive so that it is not to be recommended even for an entirely "crackle"-free batik design.

Any wax skimmed off during the de-waxing process cannot be re-used as it is rather brittle, and the water residue can cause it to splutter and spurt outside the pan when reheated. Never wax when the material is wet: if there is the slightest hint of moisture the wax will not adhere properly whatever its quality.

It does not much matter what material the waxing-pan is made of but a thick-bottomed saucepan (or frying-pan for printing blocks) is better than a thin one as it is better balanced and keeps the wax at a more constant temperature. The sides should not be too high as this makes more work when block printing. It is essential for the pan to have a close-fitting lid that can quickly be replaced and used as an extinguisher should the wax catch fire. Normally there should not be any very great fire risk as the thick smoke given off just before combustion-point is reached gives ample warning. If waxing is carried out at the optimum temperature of between 120 and 140 °C (see "Correct wax temperatures" below) the smoking should be barely perceptible and the risk of fire almost non-existent. A thermometer fixed to the side of the pan measuring up to 170 °C is a further check. An experienced waxer can tell immediately on application whether the wax is at the right temperature and therefore need not worry about smoking or the risk of fire. The wax should, however, never be left on the heat unattended, even for a second—accidents can so easily happen.

From the fire-risk angle an electric hot-plate is safer than an open flame; if you are using the latter an asbestos mat makes for greater safety. The waxing-pan should not be placed near curtains or other inflammable material.

Do not use too great a heat when melting the wax as the material near the edges and at the bottom of the pan will melt and become overheated long before the mass in the center is ready (this will result in smoking and ultimately in a poorer quality wax).

If you use the edge of the pan for wiping the brush, wax will trickle down and spread over the hot-plate. A way of avoiding this is to stretch a wire across the top of the pan and use this to remove excess wax from the brush. A piece of aluminum foil laid between the hot-plate and the pan can also be helpful. Another way (but not on an open flame) is to wind a piece of cloth around the outside of the pan to take the drips.

## Correct wax temperatures

The melting-point of wax varies somewhat but it is usually between 35 and 50 °C. The ideal waxing temperature is somewhere between 120 and 140 °C, at which point the wax should be smoking very slightly. If the wax is hotter than this it will be too fluid to penetrate the material properly. Too great a heat also destroys the fat content and the wax becomes brittle as it is the fat that gives the wax its elastic properties. Any increase in the volume of smoke means that the fat is being consumed. Any frothing of the wax as it touches the fabric is a further sign that it is too hot. Wax catches fire at 170 to 180 °C, and the lid should always be at hand so that it can be replaced on the pan instantly to extinguish the flame if the wax starts to burn. *Never* pour water on the flames!

Remember that wax cools quickly so that even if the temperature of the melted wax is right it must immediately be applied to the material. There will be no time to ponder at length! For the same reason whatever you use to apply the wax—brush, or printing block—warm it in the wax before use —and remember that it will also cool between dippings. If the wax is too cool a yellowish-white crust forms on the surface of the material. As this tends to fall off during the dyeing process and as it has not had time to penetrate properly it must be scraped off and new wax applied. The old wax unfortunately leaves a thin film which slows up the new waxing and makes it more difficult. So, if you want to save time in the end, frequent dipping must be the order of the day.

If you have a thermometer which measures up to 170 °C the wax temperature can be more easily controlled. The thermometer must not be allowed to touch either the sides or the bottom of the pan. It can be fastened on to the edge with wire, pipe-cleaners or a clothespin. Thermostatically controlled electric hot-plates are excellent for heating wax.

### Faulty waxing

If the wax has been wrongly applied first of all gently remove as much of it as possible, both on the front and on the back, with the aid of a blunt penknife or similar implement. Then rub the remainder with a rag slightly moistened with white spirits. A cloth should also be placed underneath. Change the rag fairly frequently. Be careful to see that the spirit does not spread out over the rest of the material removing wax which does not need to be removed. It is best to take action immediately, but even so the treatment usually needs to be repeated several times with short intervals between each application. The material must be absolutely free from wax if the dye is to penetrate properly. Wherever any wax remains, however little, a lighter mark will show up after dyeing. Hence it is most important to go on rubbing until you are quite sure that no wax remains at all.

### Cracking

During the dyeing process the waxed surface of the material cracks very easily, especially if it is squeezed or compressed into too small a tub. If the wax does crack, the dye can penetrate through to the material and the pattern of cracks thus resulting can spoil the whole design. On the other hand the cracks can become part of the pattern, especially if their distribution is controlled. If the waxed surface is given a hard pinch it will produce a network of fine lines, or stars, diagonal lines, rays or any number of patterns. In this way more fine detail can be introduced into the work. Intentional splitting of the wax is usually most successful if carried out just before the final dyeing though, of course, if the cracking is to be in the first dye color it must be tackled earlier and the cracks waxed over before any further dyeing is carried out. It is easier to produce sharply defined cracks if (i) a little extra paraffin-wax is added to the wax mixture; (ii) the surface of the material is made more brittle by cooling it a little; (iii) the material is given a rather thicker wax coating.

Handle the material carefully at all times during dyeing and rinsing; even if a certain amount of cracking is intended it is best to avoid chance-made cracks. The material should not be folded between dyeings but wrapped around a roll of newspapers—cracks along the creases are to be avoided.

If cracking is to be made before the first dyeing takes place remember that this first "untreated" surface is extra hard and will need extra pressure to crack. Each dyeing makes the surface progressively more brittle and the wax easier to crack.

## Retouching between dyes

The waxed areas which are to be dyed several times must be retouched between dips to prevent too much cracking. Using too cold a wax will cause flaking—and these loosened sections must be scraped off and re-waxed. Sometimes this can best be done by applying the heated tip of a small knife to the loose fragments. Larger areas can be similarly treated but for these a small soldering-iron will be needed.

## Waxing of collars, sashes and trimmings

The quickest way of waxing a material all over is to dip it in the waxing-pan, holding it with clothespins at each end. Agitate the material to and fro in the pan for 10 to 15 seconds then take it out and "drain" it over the pan. Keep moving the material while the wax is hardening to ensure an even distribution of wax over the entire surface. If large articles are being waxed in this way spread a newspaper beside the pan to catch the drips.

**Dark outlines accentuate the design** In most batik designs the pattern will stand out sharply if it is given a darker outline. It follows from this that at each waxing care should be taken not to wax the entire surface but always to leave a narrow $\frac{1}{25}$ inch wide border which will then take all the dyes used.

*Painters can apply the wax "artist fashion."*

# Brush batik

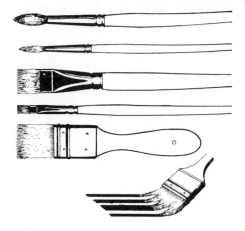

*These types of brush are all suitable for waxing. Brushes with top-quality bristles are the best; softer hair brushes are particularly good for waxing fine-spun materials.*

Large-patterned batik designs needing large waxed areas are generally best executed in brush batik, using a broad brush. Before starting work with the broad brush, however, it is a good idea to use a much smaller one for the outlines as it is difficult to paint these accurately with a broad brush. The more finely detailed the pattern the smaller the brush needed. It is often best to use a tjanting for outlining, and the brush for filling in. This is the speediest and the most professional way.

Use good-quality brushes: cheap ones will become "spiky." The brush-heads should be long (hair or bristle) so that they can draw up as much wax as possible and thus slow down the hardening process. As a general rule a stiff bristle brush is better than a soft hair brush because it will work the wax more vigorously into the material. However, a good round-ended hair brush with its fine, flexible point can make both fine and broad lines—and is particularly recommended for fine-spun materials such as Japanese silk. Apart from this there is very little difference between round and flat brushes, except that a round brush is better for making curved lines while a flat brush covers large areas more quickly and effectively. On really large areas paste-brushes can be used.

Brushes should be correctly used to avoid "spiking"—spiky bristles interfere with effective waxing. If necessary such damaged bristles should be cut. The tip of the brush may be reconditioned by stroking the bristles repeatedly against a kitchen hot-plate or an iron. Never leave a brush to harden in wax—this will deform it permanently. A new brush should be impregnated thoroughly with wax before use to give it a protective coat which should prevent spiking through overheating. This is best done by dipping the brush in the waxing-pan a couple of times while the wax is still melting and not too hot. Always make brush-strokes in the direction of the hairs, never against them. Never leave wax-impregnated brushes anywhere where they will adhere to the surface when the wax begins to harden. Finally, never bend a wax-impregnated brush as this will break the bristles.

For best results do not allow the material to touch the under-layer while waxing is proceeding. To avoid this place weights on top of the material and hold up the part to be waxed in the left hand. Another effective and much-used method is to stretch the material over a wooden frame. Artists' collapsible stretcher frames are excellent for the purpose. They can be bought in various sizes and several, of varying measurements, can be arranged to meet different requirements. A disadvantage of such frames is that they are normally rather bulky—and if several workers are grouped around the waxing-pan there will not be enough room to work. Another snag is that the thumb tacks leave unsightly marks behind, especially in the case of tightly stretched fine materials. Moreover, if the pattern is not drawn on the material and the edges of the frame are used to provide the necessary guide-lines the design can go very much askew where the fabric has not been fastened running with the weave.

A firm underlay will facilitate and speed up waxing—a $\frac{1}{4}$ to $\frac{1}{2}$ inch thick foam-rubber sheet is effective and easy to use: it will stop the material from slipping and allow the wax to penetrate right through the material, and can be used a number of times. Plastic or waxed paper can also be used for the purpose, if it is fastened with Scotch tape ("Sellotape") to the underlay.

When applying the wax it is essential to see that it is spread evenly. If it is not, the dye will penetrate the fabric to a greater or lesser extent at various points. Check that the wax is warm enough (see "Correct wax temperatures" on page 41) and, for an even flow, do not brush too fast or too slowly as you apply the wax. Dip the brush frequently in the wax. If the waxed surface of the material no longer looks like amber the wax has been allowed to grow too cold. Usually it is better to brush the wax on twice on the right side and then touch up the reverse side where necessary. The dye is otherwise apt to penetrate from the wrong side. If especially thick material is used it may even be necessary to wax over the whole of the reverse side. The brush-strokes will not leave any marks if the wax coating is the right thickness. On the other hand, if the wax is touched up brush-strokes usually show wherever there are two layers of wax.

Poorly executed waxing often shows up the beginner (see

illustration below). Here you can see horizontal, vertical, diagonal and circular brush-strokes. In places the wax has been too hot and, therefore, applied too hastily with the result that the wax coating is too thin; in others the wax has been allowed to become too cool so that the wax has been applied too thickly. Also, at the beginning of each brush-stroke too much wax has adhered to the material. With luck, of course, such haphazard work may have a charm all its own—but anyone who wishes to produce such effects deliberately must needs be a very skilful waxer.

**Brush patterns** Cut away small sections of a $1\frac{1}{2}$ to $3\frac{1}{2}$ inch wide brush, so that three to four strokes can be painted simultaneously. The gaps between each tuft, and the size of these, can be varied (see illustrations on page 44 and opposite).

**Semi-transparent wax** If the first waxing gives a thin coat then the dye will only penetrate the material slightly. If this is then re-waxed after the dyeing with an equally thin coat, and the material is then dipped in another color, the blend of colors so produced will be considerably paler than those of any unwaxed area. The whole art in this case consists in making firm brush-strokes with no overlapping to avoid streaks wherever the wax is in two layers. The brush used must be a pretty broad one and most of the wax must be cleaned from it before it is applied with comparatively rapid strokes, as only the minimum of wax should adhere to the material.

The wax should not be too hot. After dyeing particular care must be taken over the sections where re-waxing has been done. If, despite care, there are places with an extra thick layer of wax, scrape off the surplus with a blunt knife (see also "Scraper technique" on page 80).

*This is a good example of work which has been poorly waxed. In some places the wax coating has been too thin and the re-waxing has been done in a very haphazard fashion.*

Opposite *Here very effective use has been made of a brush with bristles cut in spikes.*

# Tjanting batik

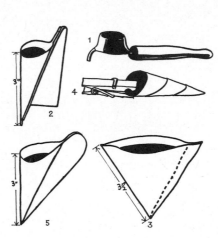

The tjanting (dropper) is used to obtain finely detailed effects in batik work. There are several varieties of tjanting but basically it is a container so constructed that the wax can be poured from it in a thin stream (see diagrams above). In southern Asia the traditional and well-proven tjanting has not changed much over the centuries. It consists of a small copper container with a short wooden handle and a very thin spout. The tip of the spout is bent slightly downward. When the container is filled with hot wax and tipped up the wax flows out of the needle-fine opening to draw fine lines on the material (see diagram 1).

Do not overfill the container or the wax will tend to spill over on to the material. When refilling the tjanting, immerse the container completely in the hot wax. This will both heat it up and melt any wax which may have cooled and hardened in the spout. To prevent any wax dropping on to the material wipe the tjanting with a piece of rag and hold the rag under the nozzle until waxing is recommenced. Keep the rag close at hand during the waxing process so that it can quickly be placed under the nozzle of the tjanting to catch the drips.

The waxed line made by the tjanting is normally about $\frac{1}{25}$ inch in width and the hole in the spout is so exceedingly small that only a very fine-gauge needle can be inserted in it. The width of the line is, however, not solely determined by the size of the opening in the spout. If, for instance, the wax is too hot it will flow more quickly along the spout so that if the tjanting is not moved quickly enough the line will become thicker. If the wax is not fluid enough it will not isolate the material sufficiently and this will result in blurred lines when the dye is applied. It is quite possible, on lifting the tjanting out of the waxing-pan, to judge whether the wax is at the right temperature or not by the rate at which the wax drops from the nozzle. It is only when the rate of flow is approximately 1 drop per second (roughly the rate of your pulse) that the moment is ripe to start work. If the line made by the tjanting is too fine, enlarge the hole in the spout gently with a fine needle. If the opening is too large, squeeze the spout very slightly (when doing this do not hold the container itself but hold on to the spout to prevent it from working loose).

Should any impurities, such as soot, slow up the flow of wax, clear the spout with a very fine wire. Many people find it useful to place a small piece of wick in the container to regulate the flow and sieve off impurities. When the tjanting is not in use make sure that the sensitive tip is not touching any spilt wax.

*This is a good example of the fine results that can be obtained with a brush.*

In Java the women sit on the ground when using a tjanting. They keep an open fire burning beside them to maintain the wax at the right temperature. The material is suspended from a pole and held in the left hand. By holding the work in this perpendicular position the risk of wax dropping on to it is eliminated. The tjanting is held between forefinger and thumb with the handle held inside the palm of the hand. When not in use the tjanting is tilted gently upwards so that the wax can no longer flow out of the spout. Tjantings vary in appearance; usually there is only one spout but occasionally there are two or even three spouts. In our part of the world we are more accustomed to spreading our work out on tables. We also find it easier to hold the tjanting more as if it were a pencil. Excellent results can be obtained using the tjanting in this way.

A beginner does not need to buy a proper tjanting as a much simpler device can be made to serve the purpose. Diagram 5 on page 48 shows a simple tjanting made of stiff paper—including the handle. It is glued together with heat-resistant glue. Diagram 4 on page 48 shows another type of tjanting that can also be made of strong paper. Glue is applied to the top edge of the paper which is then rolled together to make a pointed cone but without any hole. When the glue has dried a hole is made in it with a fine needle and a clothespin clipped on to form the handle. The paper tjanting illustrated in diagram 3 is made from a $2\frac{1}{2}$ inch long corner cut from a triangular carton (for example, a milk or orange-juice carton). A tiny hole is pierced in the point and the broad glued section is cut off at an angle to form a point while the other end of this makes an excellent handle.

For best waxing results using the tjanting on a table stretch the material over a frame and do not allow it to touch the underlay. It is easier for beginners, however, to use a foam-rubber underlay under the material and this method can also give excellent results. You may find it helpful when making borders to isolate the boundary-lines with Scotch tape ("Sellotape") or newspaper to prevent any wax going over the edges.

Designs made with a tjanting are usually easily distinguishable. The whole composition is built up in a manner appropriate to the particular technique, using spirals, zigzag lines as well as dots and tear-drop shapes, all of which can be highly decorative. Tjanting-users need not be daunted by the thought of covering even quite large areas. An efficient implement will reduce the time taken over the work and it need not take too long. Even a plain wax-covered surface can provide scope for simple patterning. By drawing the tjanting across the material horizontally or vertically a very slight striping effect is produced. Drawing both vertically and horizontally gives a light check. A series of curlicues will give another attractive design (see examples opposite).

*Background patterns made with a tjanting.*

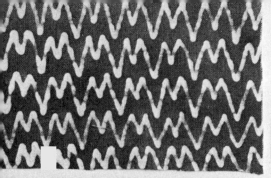
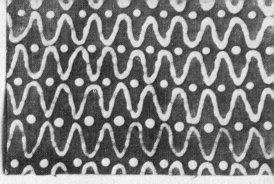
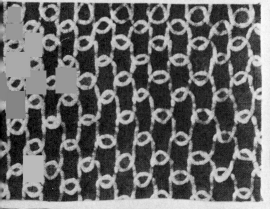
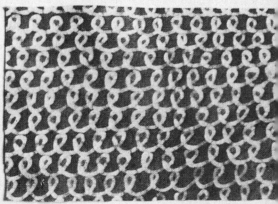

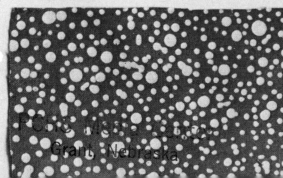

# Printing block batik

Printing block batik is the quickest method of producing waxed patterns: it is fun to do and exciting, so just for a change why not give it a trial? The Javanese produce really attractive work using this technique but even if our own productions cannot compare with theirs it is nevertheless possible to make truly satisfying textiles with very primitive printing blocks. Use your imagination to think up new items that may be used —batik printing blocks are not commercially available.

Cardboard tubing, for instance, can be molded to form suitable printing blocks and indeed any stiff card will serve the purpose (for examples see opposite). Printing blocks that are sturdy enough to be practical should not be more than 2 to $2\frac{1}{2}$ inches high. Make them identical on both sides, including the bit that is held. This can be reinforced with Scotch tape ("Sellotape") to help keep its shape. The printing surface must be absolutely flat—any excrescences will ruin its efficacy.

Pipe-cleaners can easily be made into serviceable printing blocks (see illustration on page 55). The fluffy part absorbs the wax and helps give a softened outline rather like brushwork— while the inner core of wire is strong and at the same time flexible. Just one pipe-cleaner can be twisted to form a small "block," complete with handle. The illustrations on page 57 show designs made out of one or more pipe-cleaners (as many as eight pipe-cleaners have been used in some designs).

*Many small odds and ends from the kitchen will make useful batik printing blocks. It is just a case of experimenting. The lower part of the picture shows blocks made from cardboard tubing and cartons.*

It is, however, generally best not to make these blocks too large—they should not be more than 2 inches long. Short-tufted pipe-cleaners are the best for the purpose. Large blocks must be pressed firmly on to the material with one hand. It helps to wear a couple of thimbles on this hand. Always begin by making small simple blocks and try these out first as they will provide valuable experience for making and using more ambitious models. Blocks made from card or pipe-cleaners are apt to lose their shape slightly in use, but this is no real disadvantage as designs so made will tend to look less stereotyped.

Simple biscuit-cutters and cake-forms are also useful, (rings, hearts and stars for example). Protect your fingers from burning by using material to insulate them. Other small odds and ends to be found in the kitchen can also be put to use (see illustrations on page 53). Root vegetables too can be made into interesting printing blocks. Wash and slice a potato or carrot into two then press the cut side on to newspaper a couple of times to rid it of unnecessary moisture. Cut out a simple design on this same side about $\frac{1}{4}$ inch deep. Avoid making designs with too great a printing surface. More uniform, sturdy printing blocks can be ordered from a copper-smith. They are best made from a minimum thickness of $\frac{1}{25}$ inch copper. Chose simple designs and fix them to wooden handles.

Printing block and brush batik can be combined effectively. It simplifies the work to use a brush to fill up the spaces between the waxed outlines and there is no risk of going over the edges. Usually the block printing is done first, the material is dipped in dye, then the brush is used to wax over larger areas and lastly the final dyeing is carried out.

Designs made using a printing block may present a rather spindly appearance but the more solid patches of color produced by the brush will help to fill out the whole. Satisfactory designs can, however, be made with blocks only, especially if several different ones are used and at least two dyes. Do not allow your block batik design to become monotonous through meaningless repetition. It is just as important to have a good basic plan determining the positioning of the dyes as to have well-designed blocks themselves (for further examples of designs see page 28).

Make a block "pad" (see illustration on page 56) by placing a thin piece of foam rubber $\frac{1}{8}$ inch thick on the bottom of a shallow tin. There should be just enough wax barely to cover the pad. If there is too much wax the blocks become overloaded and the spreading out of the wax will make the designs coarse-looking. Blocks with a printing surface of $\frac{1}{2}$ to 1 inch square or more do not absorb enough wax from a pad of this kind, however, and must be immersed in the waxing-pan itself to a depth of about $\frac{1}{4}$ inch. Scrape the surplus wax off on to the edge of the pan a few times, or alternatively scrape the inside of the block itself. Block batik requires a rather lower wax temperature than the brush or tjanting technique. If the wax is too hot it will spread and make the pattern coarse and the wax layer on the material will also be too thin. The block should be held in position over the material for 5 to 10 seconds otherwise the wax coating will not be strong enough to withstand the dye.

It is important to ensure when printing that the blocks are warm enough. It is not enough that the wax is hot: used cardboard and pipe-cleaner blocks always have a residue of wax and this must be allowed to melt. The kind of saucepan normally used for melting wax is not very suitable as the sides are too high, but a thick-bottomed stew-pan is ideal. It keeps the wax at a more constant temperature and stands firmly.

Prepare your work-table before starting to print. Place a

layer of foam rubber $\frac{1}{4}$ to $\frac{1}{2}$ inch thick on the table under the material. Make sure the material to be printed is absolutely smooth and unwrinkled. Before printing mark out clearly where the design is to come, and where the blocks are to be placed (see also "Transferring the design" on page 34). Block printed batik designs do not as a rule have particularly thick wax coats so that the dye usually penetrates a little. If the wax covers the material reasonably smoothly the appearance of the fabric is even enhanced somewhat as the color contrasts are not as strong. If several dye baths are to be given then for safety's sake it is best to brush on a little wax after the first dyeing over places where the wax looks thinnest.

*This collection of pipe-cleaner printing blocks should provide inspiration.*

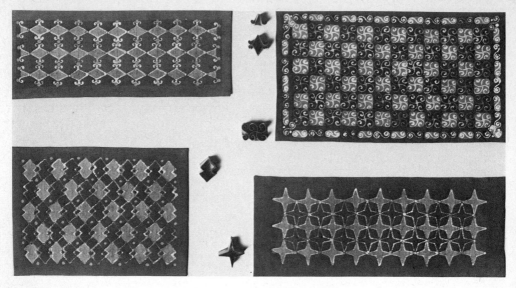

*Here the designs have been waxed on with blocks made of very thin card. For fine lines like these a printing pad must be used.*

These blocks are made out of the same sort of card but as they have a larger printing surface they can be dipped in the waxing-pan.

Opposite *These designs have been made with pipe-cleaner printing blocks. Some areas have then been waxed over with the help of a brush.*

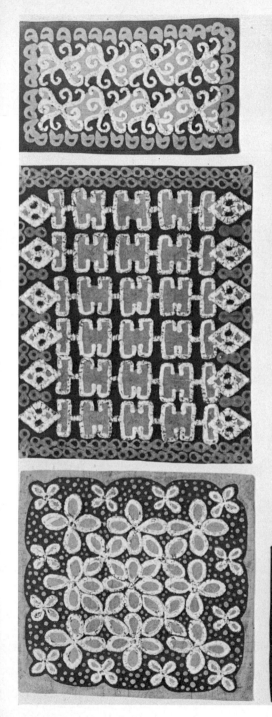
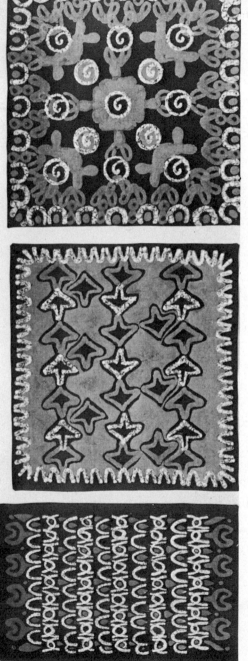

It is always exciting to find out how the printing block works in practice. Retouching is sometimes needed, so that either the block is stamped on again or some small area is repainted with the wax brush. The waxing-pan can be seen on the right.

# Stencil batik

Most people have some idea of how to use a stencil when painting but very few have tried adapting the technique to wax batik (see illustration on page 60). We live in an age of plastics and this means, *inter alia*, that preparations such as "Contact" or "Fablon" may be used to make self-adhesive stencils which are very suitable for batik work. "Contact" consists of a thin plastic film, one side of which is adhesive and protected by a layer of paper. It is most often used for covering shelves, boxes and so on. It can be bought by the yard at a reasonable price in a wide range of colors with or without a design. Transparent plastic is preferable as this makes it easier to see that the stencil has been correctly placed on the material. Not all brands of plastic coating are equally suitable for use as stencils, and it is therefore wise to buy small amounts first and experiment a little. Stencils made from *any* brand, however, do not work really well until they have been used four or five times. It is best to buy a brand which has backing paper marked in squares (pure white is obtainable) as this makes it easier to cut straight. The squares also help in the cutting out of stencils, especially if the design has been created on square paper ruled to the same scale. Cut the stencils with small embroidery- or nail-scissors, or with a stencil-cutter. Do not remove the backing paper until the stencil is ready or the plastic will stick to the fingers and anything else with which it comes in contact. Once the stencil is ready, then remove the backing paper and apply the stencil to the material, which will already have been marked out (see also "Transferring the design" on page 34).

When your stencils are not in use keep them stuck on a piece of plastic. After a stencil has been used for a couple of waxings it may acquire an awkwardly thick layer of wax on its surface. If it does, wait until the wax has hardened then scrape it off. A stencil can often be used for as many as thirty to fifty waxings if the material to which it has been applied is not too fluffy.

Work carefully. Remember (i) not to take too much wax on the brush; (ii) not to paint too rapidly over the stencil; (iii) not to make the wax too hot. Unless these three rules are observed the wax will only too easily find its way under the stencil. Do not lose heart if the first few attempts are not too successful as plastic needs a little time to acquire the right thickness of wax and the correct touch is soon acquired.

As to the form of the stencils themselves, these should not be too large or too small and they should be simple. As far as possible the contours of the stencil should be all of a piece with no extraneous bits. The latter tend to stick awkwardly and hinder the transfer of the stencil. Page 61 shows good examples of suitable designs. It is quite possible, using the same stencil, to produce many delightful variations on the same design—by, for instance, turning it to face the other way or repeating the pattern to make interesting groups.

An attractive effect is produced by first stenciling the design on to the material, dyeing, then reapplying the stencil to the material but shifting it very slightly, then re-waxing and re-dyeing. Another satisfactory method is to use different stencils for the same piece of fabric in conjunction with two or more dyes. Stencil batik is particularly suited to the use of repeat patterns, saving, as it does, a great deal of time.

*Some examples of stencil batik.*

*These patterns will
provide plenty of ideas
for stencil batik.*

# Dyes and dyeing

There are many types of dye on the market but very few textile dyes. Most of those available can, however, be used for hand-printing and painting on fabric as well as for dyeing the entire work.

**Vat dyes** These are the most color-fast and have the widest and richest color range. Most will dye cold and can, therefore, be used for batik work (a dye requiring too hot a temperature would melt the wax) but they are expensive, and have various disadvantages. First, they are quite complicated to prepare and once prepared require constant attention. Then the chemicals used with them (sodium hydrosulphite; caustic soda) can burn the skin and must be kept out of reach of young children. The process also requires a lot of space— which not many people have to spare—and, finally, the choice of material is limited to natural fibers (cotton, linen, batiste, silk and so on).

**Multipurpose and liquid instant dyes** These come in a wide range of colors and can be used on most fabrics. Unfortunately, they have only limited color-fastness and though most can be dyed cold, only a hot dye produces a good depth of color. They are, therefore, not eminently suitable for serious batik work, although attractive pastel effects can be achieved. They are, however, good to start on, particularly for children.

**Cold-water "reactive" dyes** These are generally the most

satisfactory for amateur batik workers. They are color-fast and withstand much hard washing, they are safe and simple to use, can be bought in a good range of colors and dye successfully at a low temperature (though *not* cold as the name suggests). They can be bought in small quantities and are relatively inexpensive. Their one main disadvantage is that, like vat dyes, they only work on natural fibers.

## Suppliers

Batik Craft Supplies, 1 Industrial Road, Woodbridge, New Jersey 07075 carries everything needed for batik work, including wax and dyes in amounts from one ounce to pound size. Saks Arts and Crafts, 1103 North Third Street, Milwaukee, Wisconsin 53203 also has special dyes for batik. Fezandie & Sperrle, Inc., 103 Layfayette Street, New York, N.Y. 10013 and Cushing Dyes, Dover-Foxcroft, Maine 04426 offer a wide selection of dyes and dyestuffs.

Dylon International Limited, 139 Sydenham Road, London SE26, will supply cold-water dyes, multipurpose dyes and liquid instant dyes in various quantities. The company also runs a helpful Consumer Advice Bureau at the same address. Skilbeck Brothers Limited, Bagnall House, 55 Glengall Road, London SE15, will supply "Caledon" vat dyes in manageable quantities.

## Preparing a cold-water dye

Whichever make you choose, always follow the manufacturer's instructions. The basic procedure, however, is always the same:

Empty the correct amount of powder into a cup and mix with salt to a gruel-like consistency (the salt helps "open up" the fabric to receive the dye). Add water at a temperature of 90 to 95 °C, being careful not to add more than the powder can take without changing color. If necessary, pour the mixture through a fine cloth to catch the undissolved particles. Fill a plastic tub or other suitable container (not zinc) with water. Add the dye solution until a suitable strength is obtained. Add ordinary household soda or a cold-water dye "fix" (to "reactivate" the dye). The solution should be at a temperature of 25 to 30 °C. Even with cold-water dyes the higher the temperature of the water the better the dye will "take," but remember that wax melts at a temperature of about 35 °C.

## Preparing a vat dye

Again, whichever make you choose, follow the manufacturer's instructions implicitly. Here is the basic procedure: Measure the correct quantity of dye powder. Mix equal quantities of cold and boiling water to make a temperature of some 55 °C. Stir in the dye, mixing it thoroughly with the water (if the powder does not dissolve completely there is a risk of adhering particles staining the fabric; this can be minimized by mixing the dry powder with a little water to a gruel-like consistency before adding the rest of the water). Stir in approximately half a teaspoon of caustic soda and half a teaspoon of sodium hydrosulphite per pint of water. Leave until the mixture drops to a temperature of about 30 °C. Once mixed, the solution should be used within the hour for best results though it is possible to reactivate the dye by replenishing the chemicals added.

### Calculating dye bath quantities

The amount of water used in the dye bath will depend on the thickness and size of the material. Medium coarse cotton of about $3 \times 3$ feet (weighing 6 to 8 ounces) is normally dyed in about 8 pints of water. For fine materials measuring about 2 or 3 feet square 1 pint will suffice. For curtains or a larger table-cloth, for example, the most practical way of proceeding is to fold it to the size of a table-mat, count the number of layers and allow 1 pint for each layer. It is not a good idea to make up a dye bath of less than 2 pints even if you are going to dye only one table-mat, as smaller quantities do not allow enough room for stirring. And in the case of vat dyes the sodium hydrosulphite is consumed too quickly if the dye bath is too small. Also, if cracking of the waxed surface is to be avoided the dye solution and the container must both be roomy. It may seem odd that large-scale batik works which are for the most part covered in wax need so large a dye bath but remember that you must be able to immerse the material completely and agitate it properly. The dye bath may, however, be made a little weaker provided that the dyeing time is increased and that the wax will stand this.

One useful method of treating large pieces of work which safeguards the wax and economizes on dye, even though the solution must be made a little stronger than normal, is to use a dyeing vessel with low sides and draw the material to and fro over the sides while dyeing.

### Trial strips

Before starting to dye it is a good idea to test timing, colors and combinations on trial strips of the material in question. These trial strips are particularly useful for comparison purposes if your work is to be given several colors because after the second dyeing the first dye will either have acquired the blend color or it will have been covered with a layer of wax— and in either case will no longer be visible. For this reason keep one trial strip for each dye at hand while the dyeing is in progress. It is also a good idea to check that the color blends of first and subsequent dyes are satisfactory. Rinse the trial strips, squeeze them out in newspapers and either iron them or dry on a hot-plate. While the strips are even slightly damp the colors are misleading. If time is short, however, a wet strip will give some approximate idea of the final outcome if it is held to the light. If the color is not quite as desired then the strength

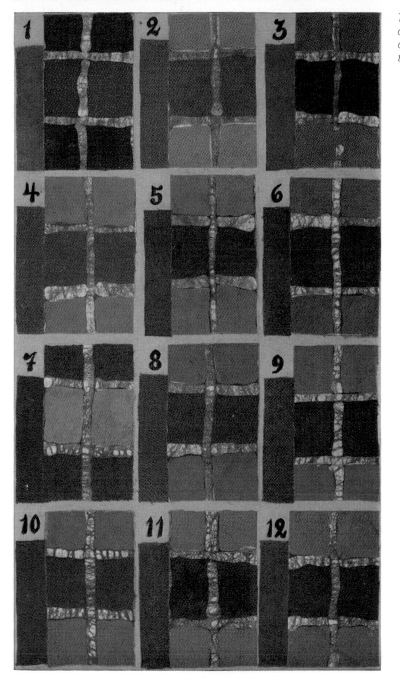

These are some of the color combinations that can be achieved using two dye baths.

These are some of the color combinations that can be achieved using three dye baths.

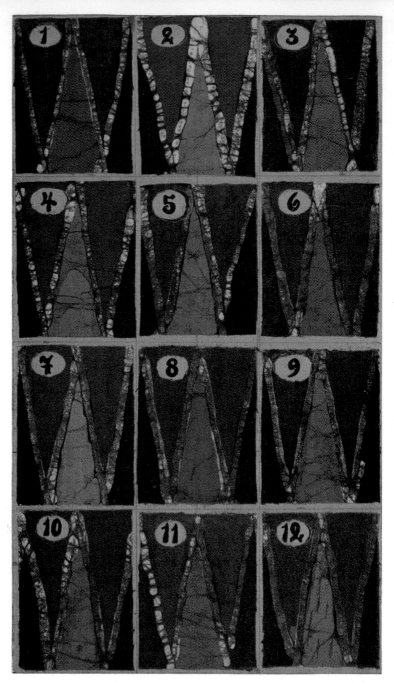

of the dye bath can be adjusted until it is right. Remember that the actual final coloring will only appear a short interval after the strip has been removed from the dye. Remember also in this connection that a number of dyes change their color slightly during boiling.

It is a good idea to keep samples from all successful dyeings with notes on the make-up of the dye and the length of the dyeing time—also on the material used, as the color obtained can vary with different types of materials. This can be very helpful. All the thrill of the collector is felt whenever any particularly fine specimen is added to the collection.

## The dyeing process

Before starting to dye, wash and soak the material in water and experiment with trial strips as described. Then, when you are ready to start, immerse the material in the dye bath for a suitable length of time (be guided by the manufacturer and by your trial strips; the minimum time for a good depth of color in a cold-water dye is about 30 minutes). Avoid keeping any part of the material doubled up for longer than necessary so that the dye has every chance to penetrate and the dyeing is as even as possible. To avoid undue cracking the material should not be squeezed and for the same reason (as already pointed out) the tub should not be too small and the dye solution should be generous. To avoid cracking altogether, use the shallow-bath technique already described and keep the material flat. This is particularly important for batik portraiture, for which disfiguring blemishes must be avoided. When the material has been dyed to the right shade, take it out of the dye bath and rinse thoroughly, preferably with tepid water, until the water runs almost clear to remove the excess dye. The color can be fixed by adding a little vinegar to the last basin of rinsing water and allowing the fabric to soak in this for about 5 minutes. Once the material has been rinsed, lay it out on newspapers to allow to drain. If the work is to be dyed again and not de-waxed it is particularly important to ensure that it is kept flat because a crumpled surface is difficult to wax. It cannot be over-emphasized that the material should be handled with the utmost care at this point and at the rinsing stage to prevent damage to the wax. After drying do not fold the material but roll it around a roll of newspapers so that there is no risk of cracking along the line of the fold (see "Retouching between dyes" on page 43).

If the work is made up of several pieces then all these should be immersed in the same dye at the same time, for even if the dye retains much of its power it is inevitable that if one half has already been dyed then the second batch will be paler as much of the dye's strength will have been used up in the first dyeing. It will not improve matters to lengthen the dyeing time in this weaker dye in the hope of obtaining a darker shade by so doing. If there are so many pieces to be dyed that it is impossible to do them all at the same time then make up enough dye solution to dye the lot, divide it into two (or more) portions and use one for each batch of dyeing. Never empty away a dye bath until you have ascertained from a fully dry trial strip of cloth that your fabric has received sufficient color for your purpose.

An attractive effect can sometimes be produced by leaving one section of the material in the dye for rather longer than the rest. Occasionally, it is possible to keep two dye baths going at the same time—for instance, if the middle section is dipped in the one bath and rinsed, then the two outer edges are dipped in the other dye, and finally, a smaller section of the material where the two colors meet is dipped in both dyes. This method of dyeing has much in common with tie-dyeing, but is only suitable for wax batik work that will tolerate being creased quite frequently to produce fairly definite lines of demarcation for the dyeing to be carried out. If it proves difficult to keep the material together, tie a piece of twine loosely around it (see also "Tie-dyeing combined with wax batik" on page 90 and "Contrast dyeing" on page 77).

Often it is unnecessary to wax and dye the whole fabric if it adapts itself to being waxed and dyed in parts only. Just wax almost up to the area to be dyed. For large pieces of work a practical method in such cases is to pack the areas which are not to be dyed in a plastic bag. For more about this method of dyeing see also "Dyeing of individual details" on page 79.

## Uneven dyeing

In the event of uneven dyeing, consider the causes of this so that a repetition can be avoided. Was the dye bath too small? Did you bundle up the material too much? Was it patchy (for instance, wax wrongly applied and not completely removed), was the fabric too crumpled or folded in such a way that it creased badly (in such instances the material is apt to fray more easily and this allows the dye to penetrate too readily). Was the material a non-iron one, with a glaze which prevented the dye from "taking" properly? Or did the material have too much dressing?

With home-dyed fabrics it is difficult to avoid a slightly rippled effect altogether and this cannot even be considered a fault exactly as it is just this lack of uniformity which constitutes the appeal of handmade textile designs. If the unevenness is worrying it can be made less noticeable if you dip the material in another color dye. Before you do this, however, wax over any areas which would be better left untreated. It is nearly always after the first dyeing that the unevenness shows up most. To keep the color unchanged one possibility is to wax over the entire surface, to crumple this well and then dip the material in a darker dye. The darker cracking so obtained breaks up and diminishes the effect of the uneven background color. If the material has one or two really bad patches and the design cannot be modified without altering it considerably, try adding a discreet under-pattern and then giving the whole thing another dyeing. One comfort is that batik often improves with further dyeings.

## Correcting the color depth

If the material appears to have absorbed too much dye the excess may be removed by soaking it in tepid soapy water for several minutes (the temperature of the water must not exceed 30 °C or the wax may melt). This soaking must be done before de-waxing takes place or the dye that has been removed will color the previously undyed areas. If the work is *still* too dark, bleaching sometimes helps to lighten the color, particularly if carried out immediately.

## One dye bath batik

1 *Material with design drawn on it.*
2 *The waxed material is ready for dyeing.*
3 *The material has been dyed yellow (the wax is still in position).*
4 *The wax has been boiled out and the work is completed.*

## Two dye bath batik

1 *The material has been waxed and dyed yellow.*
2 *The areas which are to remain yellow have been waxed.*
3 *The material has been dyed blue.*
4 *The wax has been boiled out and the work is completed.*

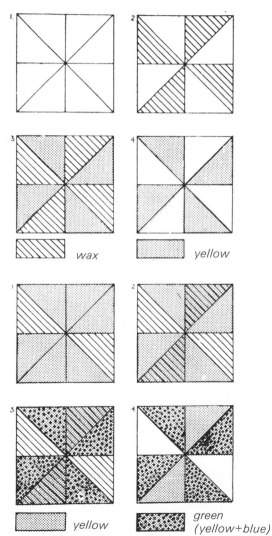

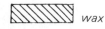

wax    yellow    green (yellow+blue)

67

## Three dye bath batik

1   The material has been waxed and dyed yellow.
2   The areas to remain yellow have been waxed and the material has been dyed blue.
3   The parts to remain green have been waxed and the material has been dyed purple.
4   The wax has been boiled out and the work is completed.

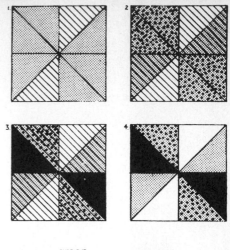

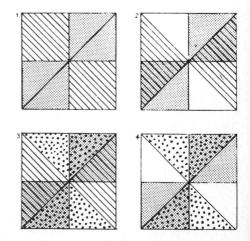

## Two dyes with the wax removed between dyeings

1   The white areas and the areas to be dyed blue have been waxed and the material has been dyed yellow.
2   All the wax has been boiled out and the areas which are to be white and yellow have been waxed.
3   The material has been dyed blue.
4   The wax has been boiled out and the work is completed.

# Color considerations

If a piece of material is to be dyed in several different colors the lightest color should be dyed first and the rest graduated according to shade—since a dark fabric cannot be made lighter (a yellow dye can, however, make a dark batik product *look* lighter). See also the diagrams on pages 67 and 68.

Material which is given two dyes will take on the first color and a blend of the first and second colors combined. Therefore in batik the second color will only show in its pure form in the cracking where the material was still white at the time of the second dyeing. Thus, if the first dye is red and the second blue, the colors when the work is completed will be red and purple.

To color a batik fabric white, red and blue, for example, take the white as the starting-point, next cover all the blue and white areas, then apply the red. The fabric is now red and white and must be de-waxed. Finally, re-wax all the areas which are to remain red and white before executing the final dipping in blue dye (it will make no difference if the work is carried out in the reverse order—that is, if the blue dip precedes the red).

If, when giving three dye baths, you wish to retain the second color in its pure form in the cracking then the color must be protected by a fresh wax coating to prevent the third dye from penetrating. If the batik is to be given more than three dyes it will always need re-waxing, remembering that after three dyeings the wax will be exceedingly brittle. Plan the waxing sequence carefully to make the most of all the possibilities of producing various tints and color blends.

In batik work the choice of color is the most important, and the most difficult question. It is very helpful, therefore, to train yourself to "think in color" before undertaking more ambitious projects. It is not worth while, in preliminary attempts, to use more than one color, but this should not be of too pale a tint. When you have mastered one-color dyeing, move on to simple projects in two or three dyes. For more advanced work using a number of dye baths consult the color chart on page 73.

### Working out colors and color blends

It helps to see how a color blend will turn out, or how it will match the existing colors, if two strips of thin material of the desired colors are crossed over one another and held up to the light. If the right color cloth is not available then thin paper strips painted the right shade in water-colors will give some idea of the outcome.

### Suitable two-dye and three-dye combinations

These are suggestions to help the beginner choose suitable colors to combine. When using these combinations make sure the first dye bath is lighter than the second dye bath throughout. For three-dye projects the third dye bath must contain the strongest color if a proper balance of color is to be kept. Batik work designed in light colors only can very easily give a washed-out or faded impression. For this reason a little finely drawn dark color is often included in a pale design. This sometimes means that more than 90 per cent of the surface must be waxed and usually in such a case use is made of cracking to heighten the effect. The suggestions are divided into four groups in accordance with the color of the second dye bath irrespective of whether there are to be two or three dye baths. Remember that in a two-dye combination the second color will dominate in the final blend as this is the strongest color. For three-dye combinations the last color is usually predominant.

### Group 1

Color accent of second dye is red

| | Dye 1 | Dye 2 | Dye 3 |
|---|---|---|---|
| a | mustard or lemon yellow | bright red | emerald green |
| b | olive green | violet red | |
| c | emerald green | violet red or bright red | |
| d | bluish green | violet red | olive green (possibly) |
| e | violet red | chestnut red | emerald or olive green (possibly) |

| | | | |
|---|---|---|---|
| f | lemon yellow | orange red | bluish green |
| g | mauve | purple | khaki |
| h | mustard yellow | chestnut red | mid blue |
| i | bluish green | magenta | mauve |
| j | emerald green | chestnut red | mauve |

## Group 2

Color accent of second dye is yellow or brown

| | *Dye 1* | *Dye 2* | *Dye 3* |
|---|---|---|---|
| a | blue gray | coffee brown | |
| b | bluish green | mustard yellow or orange yellow | violet |
| c | mauve | coffee brown | |
| d | red violet | egg yellow | mauve |
| e | coffee brown | lemon yellow | violet red or emerald green |
| f | emerald green | coffee brown | mauve |
| g | violet | egg yellow | dark brown |
| h | orange red | lemon yellow | blue black |
| i | mauve | mustard yellow | red black |
| j | lemon yellow | coffee brown | gray blue |

## Group 3

Color accent of second dye is yellow

| | *Dye 1* | *Dye 2* | *Dye 3* |
|---|---|---|---|
| a | violet red | bluish green or olive green | violet (possibly) |
| b | chestnut red or coffee brown | bluish green or emerald green | |
| c | orange red | olive green | bluish green |
| d | bluish green | olive green | violet red (possibly) |
| e | lemon yellow | bluish green or olive green | violet or purple (possibly) |
| f | magenta | khaki | mauve |
| g | chestnut red | olive green | bluish green |
| h | mauve | emerald green | red black |
| i | olive green | bluish green | violet red |
| j | orange red | emerald green | mauve |
| k | lemon yellow | khaki | gray blue |

## Group 4

Color accent of second dye is blue

| | *Dye 1* | *Dye 2* | *Dye 3* |
|---|---|---|---|
| a | chestnut red | mid blue or violet blue | |
| b | coffee brown | mid blue or violet blue | |
| c | mustard yellow or olive green | violet blue | |
| d | lemon yellow | gray blue | chestnut red (possibly) |

71

| e | coffee brown | gray blue | mid blue |
| f | mustard yellow | bluish green | purple |
| g | khaki | mauve | dark green |
| h | bluish green | mauve | dark chestnut |
| i | orange red | mid blue | emerald green |
| j | magenta | gray blue | khaki |

# Color chart

The chart is based on the three primary colors: red, yellow and blue (see opposite). If you choose two related colors for your project the color chart will indicate the resulting color blend. "Related" colors are those which lie within any one third of the circle, for example, yellow or orange, yellow and green or yellow and blue. Bear in mind, however, that in a color blend in which one dye is stronger than the other the stronger color will predominate.

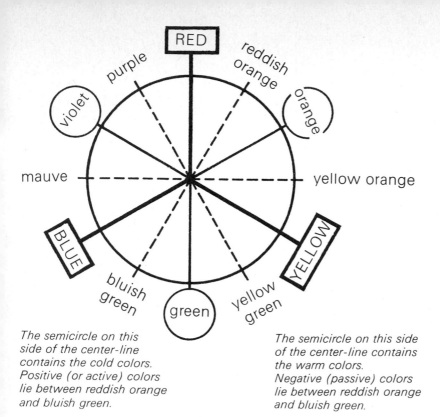

The semicircle on this
side of the center-line
contains the cold colors.
Positive (or active) colors
lie between reddish orange
and bluish green.

The semicircle on this side
of the center-line contains
the warm colors.
Negative (passive) colors
lie between reddish orange
and bluish green.

Primary colors: red, yellow, blue
Secondary colors: orange, green, violet
Color blends are colors containing at least two of the
primary colors. As each of the three sectors which lie
between the circle's three primary colors is divided into four,
nine color blends in all are obtainable from this.
Complementary colors are those which harmonize with one
another.

## How to determine complementary colors
(applicable to any part of the circle)

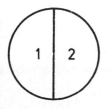
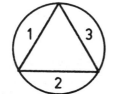
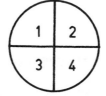

two colors          three colors          four colors          six colors          73

# De-waxing

## Boiling

The simplest way of removing wax from the material is to boil it, though not until at least 30 minutes have elapsed after the final dyeing—and always assuming the dye is color-fast and can be boiled. Both vat dyes and cold-water dyes can be boiled, the multipurpose "household" dyes on the other hand cannot. Place the finished work in a pan (any metal) large enough to hold plenty of water so that the material does not have to be bundled up too much. To each pint of water add about 1 dessertspoon of soapflakes or a mild detergent. Do not use washing detergents as these will weaken the colors.

The wax melts properly when the water reaches a temperature of 50 to 70 °C and floats up to the surface where it can be skimmed off (see illustration opposite). Agitate the material constantly and evenly to open up the layers in different places as this is the only way to loosen the wax enough for it to reach the surface. If you have not got a large utensil and the batik to be de-waxed consists of a number of items then boil each piece separately. The boiling water may be re-used each time, even if it needs additional soap and water. A very large piece of batik with an extensive wax coating may need to be boiled twice in a soap solution.

After de-waxing, rinse the material until the water runs clear.

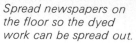
Spread newspapers on the floor so the dyed work can be spread out.

The simplest way of de-waxing a color-fast batik is to boil it in soap solution. The wax melts and rises to the surface where it can be skimmed off.

If any wax still remains it can be brushed off as this is usually little lumps which have been caught up between the layers of material and hardened during the rinsing process. If any wax *still* remains it can easily be removed if rubbed with a piece of rag dipped in a cleaning solvent.

If you only have a small pan and the batik itself is large then rinse it first in a cleaning solvent to loosen the wax. Many people, in fact, prefer to squeeze out any work in a cleaning solvent before boiling. The wax sinks to the bottom and the solvent is preserved for future use.

### Ironing

Another method of removing wax is to iron it away. Place the batik between newspapers (use old ones as the latest issue might smudge the material with printer's ink), iron, change the newspapers, iron and so on until all the wax is removed. The wax may leave some troublesome dark lines behind but these will disappear if the fabric is dipped in a cleaning solvent. Note: if you have used vat dyes, ironing by itself is not enough: the material must be boiled for 5 to 10 minutes in soapy water to fix the color as well as remove the excess dye and chemicals.

### Cleaning solvents

Alternatively, if the work cannot be boiled, the wax can be removed by immersing the work in a cleaning solvent (again, this does not apply to vat-dyed work). If a white spirit solvent affects the dye then try a dry-cleaning benzine or tetra-chloride preparation. In this case, because of the serious fire risk involved, the de-waxing should be done out of doors and the material hung up to dry until the smell has gone. Once the benzine has loosened the wax, pour it back into the bottle for re-use. Simpler still—take your work to the dry cleaners.

### Cleaning up the boiling-pan

Do not empty the dregs down the sink as they may harden and block up the pipes. Pour them into a milk carton or plastic bag which can then be thrown away. Alternatively, wait until the water is cold, remove the wax crust and pour away the water, then reheat the pan and wipe it well with news-papers. After a further wash it can be put back into ordinary household use. The wax itself cannot be re-used because of its water and soap content.

# Advanced batik

It is one thing to understand the techniques of wax batik—
it is quite another to put theory into practice. Instructions,
hints and advice have all been set out, dangers have been
listed and tricks for overcoming difficulties explained. It does
not necessarily follow from this that you will produce truly
worth while batik designs. It is only after the beginner stage
has been left behind that you will begin to evolve an individual style and to create rather than copy. This chapter is for
those who have decided that batik is their *métier* and wish
to pursue the technique further, paying a more professional
attention to detail.

## Contrast dyeing

Obviously, one end of a piece of fabric will be lighter than the
other end if one end is taken out of the dye bath before the
other. Nevertheless, this method of dyeing is rarely applied to
batik, though it is useful for dyeing skirts, curtains and wall-
hangings. If the middle of the fabric is lifted out first then both
the outer edges will be darker than the rest. If the ends are
lifted first then the middle will be darker, and so on. If the
material is dipped into several different dyes, many changing
effects can be produced by varying the shade, not least from
the multiple color blends that can result. Such contrast dyeing
can be of value also to those engaged in hand-textiles who

may wish to dye the background material in this fashion before printing is embarked upon.

### Designs drawn on waxed surfaces

It is difficult, often, to avoid waxing a narrow line unintentionally where the line lies between two areas that are being waxed. The veining on a leaf, the outline around an eye, or a signature, can, through carelessness or oversight, be brushed over. Where this has occurred it is possible to re-draw the line with the help of a darning-needle or blunt-pointed embroidery-needle. The material should be laid on newspapers and the line should be repeatedly scratched in, both on the back and the front until all the wax along the surface of the line has been removed. Do it gently and *do not use a sharp point* or you may make a hole in the material. This scratch technique can also be used for finely etched designs. A similar method is used in Javanese batik for making a pattern of close-set holes.

### Decorative wax painting

The trained artist or draftsman has a steady hand. His technique can be copied to some extent, in waxing, to produce a freer, more sensitive line. An outline which has been filled in with a free hand and *not* precisely and mechanically will impart a lighter, more individual feeling to the batik. Excellent examples of this type of work are shown on pages 85, 88, 89.

### Wax finishes

Wall-hangings, decorative cloths and similar textiles of a more

*Both these cloths were dyed green after the pattern had been dripped on. The wax was scraped off and more wax was dripped over the surface. Finally, the material was creased umbrella-fashion from the center and the point so formed was dipped in orange dye and the outer edges were dipped in a mauve dye deep enough to leave only a ring of the green.*

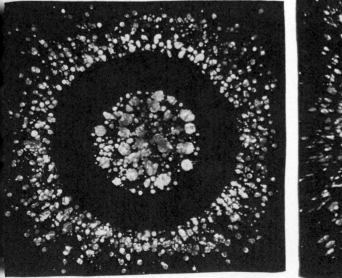
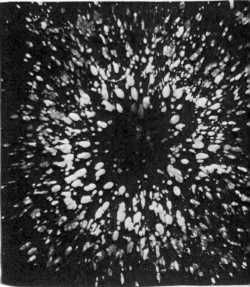

formal character acquire greater depth and a finer play of color if, after de-waxing, the surface is left lightly waxed. For this purpose leave some traces of wax when de-waxing, then, when the fabric is dipped in a cleaning solvent, a thin, all but invisible layer of wax is left covering the entire surface. When the material is placed on a layer of newspaper and ironed the whole acquires a polish in rather the same way as a floor is polished. If insufficient wax is left the same effect is obtained by lightly rubbing over the surface with a wax candle and then ironing.

*If only a small area of a fabric is to be given a certain color, the dyeing and waxing can be reduced by only waxing the areas nearest the material to be dyed, then dipping the material only as far as the outermost edge of the waxed area.*

## Dyeing of individual details

If a single detail in a piece of batik is to be given a pastel coloring it is hardly worth while dipping the whole fabric in this color. First, complete and de-wax the rest of the work *then* deal with the individual section, which will have been waxed during all the earlier dyeings. To do this, first cover the adjacent sections with wax. Then dye the section itself either by dipping it in a dish of concentrated dye (see adjacent illustration) or else painting over repeatedly while it is spread out on a piece of foam rubber or newspaper. After dyeing, squeeze the wax out in a cleaning-solvent solution (rather than repeating the laborious boiling process).

Occasionally, it is best to dye this detail first of all, before the rest of the dyeing is undertaken. If this is the case the adjoining areas must be waxed, and they must be white, though an exception might be made in the case of a marguerite, for instance, with a yellow center, white petals and a blue background. As the white petals will already have been waxed the yellow dye can be applied first. When this has been waxed over in turn the whole thing is dipped in the blue dye. Sometimes a detail must be dipped in the first dye, not into the second dye but in a third dye of quite a different color. In that case also it is best to color in the detail as soon as the fabric has been given the first dyeing.

## Background effects

A completely evenly colored background tends to seem uninteresting. If the material is first of all dyed one color, then given some unobtrusive patterning, for instance dots, and then dipped once more in a dye of a related color the general effect will be to bring the material to life and impart a uniform richness, although in reality it will be made up of several colors. A discrete design of this kind heightens the effect of the background (by using two contrasting colors a more interesting effect is produced). The simplest way of breaking up a background is to give it a slight "wax rain." This is done by brushing the wax-filled bristles of a stiff brush quickly and vigorously against, for instance, the left-hand finger (which should be protected from the hot wax with a strip of rag) at a distance of some 10 inches or so away from the material. The wax will splatter out over the surface of the fabric in a fine rain. By making this spray more or less intensive a varying background can be obtained (see further examples of background patterning on page 51 and in the final section "More batik methods" on page 90).

## Scraper technique

Varying shades from one color can only be produced by waxing and scraping. This also gives an expressive and decorative background (see illustration below) owing to the multiple, almost invisible streaks of color penetrating into the undyed background. First wax the sections you wish to keep a lighter color in the usual way, then scrape away the wax from back and front with a blunt knife. Depending on how effective the scraping is, the treated section will be up to threequarters as light again as the unwaxed sections. Where the fabric has been dyed several times the wax is so brittle that it may be preferable to rub rather than scrape it away.

One more method of preventing the dye from "taking" fully is to wax before dyeing the areas to be kept only half, or quarter as intensely colored as the rest, then rub off the greater portion of the wax with a rag moistened in a cleaning solvent. The skill here lies in removing just the right amount of wax.

*For this picture the whole surface was first waxed over, then the wax was scraped away in certain places so that the dye could penetrate.*

*Modern Indian batik illustrating* the myth of the goddess of death. *When the god Brahma created mankind he did not create death at the same time. So the earth became over-populated. The earth goddess could no longer carry this burden and complained to Brahma. He then, from his own body, created the lotus which gave birth to the goddess of death. She, however, grieved to think of the purpose for which she had been created. She wept and as her tears fell each tear drop became a different form of death—death from fire, from falling trees, from snake-bite and so on. Thus death appeared on earth in all these different forms.*

*"The Princess in the owl-haunted wood."*

# Batik as an art form

Batik can be a simple product of leisure-time activity, or it can be a work of art. As always it is difficult to draw the line between a useful art and art for art's sake. This chapter shows some of the styles and techniques adopted by various artists using different batik techniques. The form of artistic expression varies from artist to artist. Some use a direct, naïve and primitive narrative form, some rely on a lyrical impulse using decoration and pastel colorings, yet others express themselves through modern abstract art, mirroring present-day trends. Individual as the various approaches may be the essential techniques are not lost sight of nor the need to visualize imaginatively the various effects that will emerge, stage by stage, in the process of creation. Working with a medium such as a color- and light-fast dye means that there must perforce be a great degree of accuracy—mistakes, for the most part, cannot be rectified later.

A good example of minutely planned batik work is "The Princess in the owl-haunted wood" (see illustration opposite). Here the distribution of the background is carefully planned, with nothing left to chance, and the figures are skilfully drawn. The artist takes full advantage of batik's decorative possibilities in breaking up the background into finely worked-out decorative images. She makes good use of the tjanting to create these essentially batik effects.

The examples on pages 83 and 88 (top left) show skilful use of the tjanting. This artist's technique is reminiscent of the engravers. She makes carefully planned sketches for each separate stage of the waxing and dyeing processes. She uses the brush, in the main, to cover the ready dyed areas which are then to be isolated during successive dyeings. Her works frequently make use of more than six dye baths. Of this artist's pictorial use of the medium one art critic commented: "the prejudice that pictures must be painted in either oils or water-colors must be well on the way out now that nearly every kind of material is used. Latterly batik has come to be more and more used purely as a means of artistic expression. The artist has developed her technique into a perfectly controlled tool with which she can obtain exquisite effects. Like wood-carving it is based on the art of elimination; the artist makes use of fine, parallel lines which fuse together into delicately modulated shades. She is even able to paint portraits and drawings from life, without in any way being constricted by the medium."

The illustration on page 88 (bottom) also shows a very individual approach. The sureness of touch in this artist's brushwork shows clearly that she has had much experience of oil-painting. She knows precisely how much wax to take up on her exceptionally broad brushes and how quickly it must be applied. Her ability to think in color produces a wide range of hues—and this despite the fact that she almost never de-waxes before completion of the whole work. Some of her color effects are obtained through this refusal to touch up earlier waxed areas, which as the work proceeds lose the wax layer to a greater or lesser extent. If she does re-wax she is

*An artist's sketch translated into batik.*

*Detail from a flower study.*

*"Congratulations."*

quite ready to use her brush in an entirely different fashion if she considers that this will produce a better effect. Her backgrounds also show careful use of the tjanting, a factor which contributes much to her individual style.

The artist of the picture above is one of Sweden's pioneers in batik. She has been particularly successful in imparting a modern, Scandinavian character to her batik while at the same time imbuing it with the radiant, unique beauty of Eastern batik.

The artist on page 88 (top right) has relied on sharp delineation of the different fields in the composition to create his effect. Each one elegantly produces its own decisive feeling of unity. The artist of the work on pages 13 (top and center), 86 (right) and 89 (bottom) produced highly individual batik. It is fragile and lyrical in tone, with something of the French *esprit*, while at the same time her patterning is in sympathy with classical Chinese lacquer-painting. Above all else it is

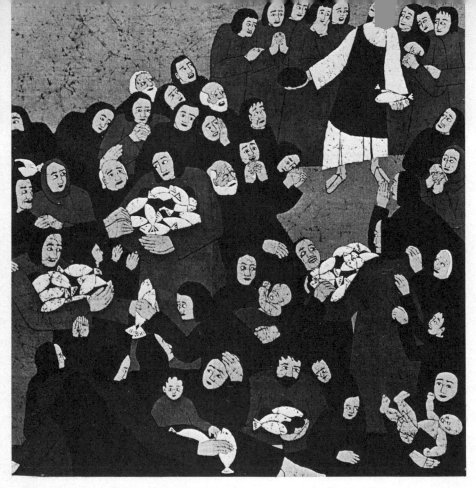

the work of a skilful draftswoman with a strong feeling for rhythm and balance. "The birch wood" on page 89 (top) is an example of work produced by someone who, from the inception of the work, can clearly visualize the finished batik. There is no suggestion here that a design has first been worked out and then translated into batik—the motif itself has arisen out of the technique.

Some batik artists like to work on a large scale covering areas several yards square. One such work, measuring some $2\frac{1}{2} \times 2\frac{3}{4}$ yards, is shown above. The theme has been taken from the Bible and the figures are drawn in simple, clear-cut lines that would be inappropriate for works of smaller dimensions. Such work could be carried out happily in tapestry or stained glass. Batik of such dimensions may need six to seven dye baths and at least one de-waxing between each dyeing. It will probably be composed and executed in two or three sections and then sewn together when completed.

*"Jesus feeds the multitude" (a work measuring some $2\frac{1}{2} \times 2\frac{3}{4}$ yards).*

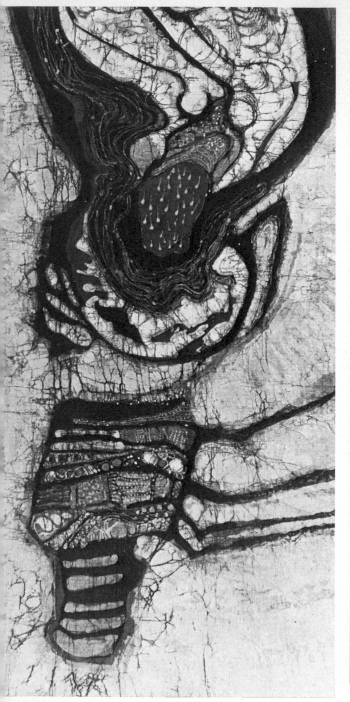

Left *"Fragment."*

Center *"Midsummer."*

*Detail from a flower study.*

A batik portrait.   "Face of a woman."

*Detail from a portrait
measuring 20×40 inches.*

*"The birch wood."*

*"The eternal triangle."*

# More batik methods

### Tie-dyeing combined with wax batik

A splendid effect can be obtained by combining the sharply defined contours of wax batik with the softer ray designs and subtle color variations of tie-dyeing (see illustrations on pages 91 and 92). First wax a design on to the material—it is of no special importance which particular technique is used. Then dye the fabric following tie-dye principles but avoiding string ties as far as possible. By combining the two methods it will only be necessary to wax before the first dye bath, even if several colors are used. Alternatively, do the tie-dyeing first and use a wax brush afterwards for painting on designs that will harmonize with the tie-dye work. Then dye the fabric once more.

A brief résumé is given here of the basic principles of tie-dyeing. These should be sufficient to make it possible to produce successful work using a combination of the two techniques. In tie-dyeing string is used to isolate the material instead of wax. The material is either folded, gathered or pleated into fine folds running either with the weave or diagonally. A check pattern is made by pleating the material then folding it at right angles to the pleats to make a square packet. A circular pattern is made by gathering the material and rolling it up like an umbrella then, beginning from the center, folding the material to produce a concentric ring

*Here the material was folded as for tie-dyeing, certain areas were dipped in wax and vigorously crumpled, then the whole material was tie-dyed.*

91

pattern, or alternatively making smaller circular pleatings more or less systematically all over the surface of the material. String is bound around the sections to resist the dye and the whole parcel is then dipped in the dye bath. String ties must be securely bound. Usually each tie is about $\frac{1}{4}$ inch wide, though occasionally ties may be as broad as 3 to 4 inches if the pattern calls for it. Designs can be varied considerably by using complicated fold patterns, different types of ties or methods of dyeing. For instance, ties can be altered between different dye baths, or selected areas can be dipped in one or more strong concentrates of dye.

*Tie-dyeing and wax batik combine well. This fabric was waxed then creased together from the center, the tip was dipped in a light turquoise dye and the remainder in mauve. Finally, the tip of the peak and the outer edges were dyed purple.*

## Paper batik

It may seem a little strange to use paper for batik designing instead of material since it takes almost as long and paper is so fragile. Paper batik has, however, a number of advantages. It is cheap, the colors used are also inexpensive and easy to work with. This means that even young children can be given the opportunity to carry out batik work in a simple and not too ambitious fashion. Paper batik is specially suitable for covering cardboard articles. It is also excellent for lampshades as the design shows up to best effect when illuminated. Use medium-thick drawing paper. If the paper is too thin it tears too easily and if it is too thick it is difficult to mount. For best results wax the design on to the paper in the same way as on to material and then color the paper with water-colors or stain applied with a brush or sponge. De-wax by ironing with the work placed between two layers of newspapers.

The easiest way of doing paper batik is to draw the design in wax crayons and then fill in the background with dark stain or water-color. A very small amount only of the color will adhere to the waxed surface and this is simple to scrape off. It is best not to paint one color over another as this smears the crayons so that the colors are no longer clear and clean looking. It is a good idea to cover most of the area leaving a narrow border so that the background stands out darkly. Remember that fine drawn lines are difficult to execute with the rather clumsy crayons.

Water will smudge a design made with wax crayons and water-color or stain, so protect it by spraying or painting on a plastic lacquer or varnish (other types of varnish are usually unsuitable). The paper itself can be strengthened by mounting it on card, "Contact," "Fablon," or some such material and binding the edges with self-adhesive plastic tape.

To give the characteristic batik "cracking" effect carefully crumple the paper before the background color is applied (if this is not done gently the paper will tear). If the paper is particularly tough it is best to try soaking it in water and then crumple it very cautiously. If you are using wax crayons try to keep the different parts of the design away from one another or the colors may smear. If on the other hand you are using a stain the whole paper can be crumpled up and dipped in this.

Attractive designs can also be made on paper using some of the methods employed in tie-dyeing. First, soak the paper in water then gently "work" it to make it malleable. Fold it while still wet and dip the edges and tips in color. As the use of this color rules out the possibility of rinsing, the dyed areas must not be dipped in another color which would result in mixing the dye bath colors. To get a fine veined effect twist and squeeze the paper so that the colors penetrate into the creases. Use rubber gloves.

When your paper batik is completed, place it on a layer of newspapers and iron the back, preferably covered with a piece of moistened paper. For a more mellow, parchment-like appearance, rub both surfaces over with paraffin and iron once more between newspapers. A stearine-wax candle can also be used but this may leave behind traces of white wax.

*Paper batik. The lampshade and paint-brush container on the left have both been tie-dyed and stained. The round containers in the center have been decorated with wax crayons and stained. The three articles on the right are wax batik and stain.*

## Batik on pure silk

Because of the shimmering texture of silk, batik executed in this material is very decorative. A fine silk scarf, a heavy silk blouse or a dress in shantung all have a real feeling of luxury about them. A lampshade of Japanese silk imparts a delightful glow to any décor because of its fine-spun texture; a soft silk cushion contributes an aura of elegant comfort. Silk may, it must be admitted, sometimes obscure the beauty of a batik design because of its dazzling sheen. One advantage of silk is that it is not necessary to rinse it through before waxing as it is not usually dressed with dye-resisting chemicals. Another advantage is that the dye penetrates the fibers easily. A disadvantage is that the hot wax can damage the fibers and for this reason silk should not be exposed to too great a heat (see waxing and design chapters). It is also expensive. Dyeing can be carried out with either vat dyes or cold-water dyes (see chapter on dyeing). Vat dyes, however, may produce a different or lighter color on silk than on cotton, and the silk will deteriorate if it is steeped too long in a vat dye bath because of the caustic soda content. Also, silk cannot be boiled, so that de-waxing must be carried out by washing it in soapy water at a temperature of 70 °C and ironing.

## Fun batik

Drip the wax from a lit stearine candle on to the material in a pattern of large and small drops. Either concentrate them in the center and gradually tail off to the sides, or arrange them in small groups, or just drip them at random. Do not dye the material itself too dark a color (try using shading as described on page 77). Scrape off the wax and then drip on some more. Dye once more. Repeat the whole process for a third time. Then de-wax.

Another variation is to hold the material at a slant so that the wax forms tear-drop shapes as it falls. By changing the direction of the slant from time to time the drops can be made to cover the entire surface facing in different directions. Start with a concentration of drops at the center and work outward, then repeat the whole process a couple of times (see page 78).

A third suggestion is to place one or more circular or square pieces of paper of suitable size on the material and drop the wax thickly all over the surface—or another good way in this case is to spray the wax on. Take a stiff bristled brush, charge it with hot wax, and then use the index finger to splatter the wax over the material (the finger should be bound with a strip of cloth). Dye. Repeat the process a couple of times altering the position of the paper patterns. De-wax.

# Index